AF228463

TRAPSHOOTING

By K. A. Artanne

— CONTENT CONSULTANTS —

Sally Stevens and Mark Stevens,
NRA Advanced Certified Shotgun
Coaches, Level 3

SportsZone

An Imprint of Abdo Publishing
abdobooks.com

abdobooks.com

Published by Abdo Publishing, a division of ABDO, PO Box 398166, Minneapolis, Minnesota 55439. Copyright © 2020 by Abdo Consulting Group, Inc. International copyrights reserved in all countries. No part of this book may be reproduced in any form without written permission from the publisher. SportsZone™ is a trademark and logo of Abdo Publishing.

Printed in the United States of America, North Mankato, Minnesota
092019
012020

Cover Photo: Vladimir Konstantinov/Shutterstock Images
Interior Photos: ARM Photo Video/Shutterstock Images, 5, 33; Tertius Pickard/ AP Images, 6; Press Association/AP Images, 9; Shutterstock Images, 10, 15, 28; Everett Historical/Shutterstock Images, 13; Al Behrman/AP Images, 16; Dan Kraker/MPR News/AP Images, 19; Red Line Editorial, 20; Vera Larina/Shutterstock Images, 23, 27; Visual Space/iStockphoto, 24; Maxim Lysenko/Shutterstock Images, 31; Andrew Carpenean/The Independent/AP Images, 34; Taylor Balkom/ Ketchikan Daily News/AP Images, 37; Historic Collection/Alamy, 38–39; Martin Rickett/PA Wire/URN:43721201/Press Association/AP Images, 41; Alexandre Kachkov/Shutterstock Images, 42; Jae C. Hong/AP Images, 45

Editor: Patrick Donnelly
Series Designer: Colleen McLaren

Library of Congress Control Number: 2019942097

Publisher's Cataloging-in-Publication Data

Names: Artanne, K. A., author
Title: Trapshooting / by K. A. Artanne
Description: Minneapolis, Minnesota : Abdo Publishing, 2020 | Series: Outdoor adventures | Includes online resources and index.
Identifiers: ISBN 9781532190520 (lib. bdg.) | ISBN 9781532176371 (ebook)
Subjects: LCSH: Trapshooting--Juvenile literature. | Clay pigeon shooting-- Juvenile literature. | Firearms--Juvenile literature. | Shooting sports--Juvenile literature. | Gunning--Juvenile literature. | Outdoor recreation--Juvenile literature
Classification: DDC 799.3--dc23

TABLE OF
CONTENTS

CHAPTER 1
THE SPORT 4

CHAPTER 2
HISTORY 8

CHAPTER 3
THE BASICS 14

CHAPTER 4
SAFETY AND GEAR 22

CHAPTER 5
GETTING INVOLVED 32

CHAPTER 6
GLOBAL COMPETITION 40

GLOSSARY 46

MORE INFORMATION 47

ONLINE RESOURCES 47

INDEX 48

ABOUT THE AUTHOR 48

THE SPORT

Maria puts in her earplugs and adjusts her safety glasses. Beside her, the four other members of her squad do the same. They approach the field.

Maria is up first. She adjusts her hat and tucks her hair behind her ears. It's a windy day, but Maria has shot in wind before. She's been practicing for this championship for almost a year. A little wind won't stop her.

She shifts her weight just slightly onto her front foot. Then she lifts her gun. She unclicks the safety. It's time.

"Pull!"

A clay disc immediately soars through the air. Maria focuses on her target and quickly pulls the trigger.

A young woman fires at a target at the shooting range.

Laetisha Scanlan of Australia reacts after winning the gold medal at the women's trap final at the Belmont Shooting Centre during the 2018 Commonwealth Games.

BANG! The target explodes. Success!

Maria smiles. When she started trapshooting just a few years earlier, she almost never hit the target. Now, after a lot of practice and patience, she has become one of her club's strongest shooters.

A SPORT FOR EVERYONE

Trapshooting is one of the three major shotgun shooting sports in the United States. The other two are skeet and sporting clays. Trapshooting, often simply called trap, is practiced all over the world. Participants use shotguns to shoot saucer-shaped targets out of the sky. Trap is growing in popularity.

Like any sport, there are many reasons people choose to participate in trap. Some people shoot because it's an activity they can do with friends and family. Others enjoy being members of clubs or teams and earning prizes. Some trapshooters compete nationally or even globally in events such as the Olympics. Regardless of the reasons, people of all ages, genders, and abilities shoot trap.

DIFFERENCES

Trap, skeet, and sporting clays are different sports. In trap, targets fly away from the shooter and come from a single machine. In skeet, targets cross the field and come from two machines. Sporting clays is played on a course with targets that move in all directions.

HISTORY

Trap is the oldest of the three major shotgun sports. Trap began in England in the late 1700s. Bird hunters created the sport to practice their shooting skills. Shooters, primarily men, used hats to trap birds for shooting practice. They would then lift the hat and shoot the bird as it flew away.

As the sport progressed, shooters began to keep the birds in traps on the ground. The traps had long cords attached. When a shooter yelled, "Pull!" trappers pulled the cord. This released the bird from the cage. Once the bird flew into the sky, the hunter would shoot. The term "Pull!" is still used by shooters today when they are ready for the release of the target.

Frank Moore was the captain of the gold medal–winning British team at the 1908 Olympic Games.

9

Targets have come a long way from the days when actual birds were used.

It wasn't long before the sport became popular in the United States. The earliest records of US trapshooting date back to 1831 from the Sportsmen's Club in Cincinnati, Ohio. As in England, American hunters shot at live birds to improve their skills. The birds were most likely pigeons or sparrows. Some people today still refer to the targets as "clay pigeons" or "birds."

CLAY PIGEONS

By the late 1800s, people began to think it was cruel to shoot birds for sport. This led to shooters experimenting with different materials for targets. They tried rubber balloons, steel, tin, and glass balls. Some of the targets were filled with feathers or fertilizer and burst on impact. Others exploded into what looked like smoke. Glass balls were the most popular of these early targets, but they weren't perfect for trapshooting. They often broke when launched. And when shooters hit them, they left behind large amounts of broken glass.

Then, in 1880, George Ligowsky created the clay target. These targets were made of clay and baked in an oven. They were very difficult to break. At first, these targets did not replace glass balls or even live birds. Instead, shooters could participate in all three types of competition. Eventually, these targets did completely replace glass balls in the sport of trapshooting.

Today's discs are much easier to break than Ligowsky's original clay targets. They are made primarily of crushed limestone and pitch, a substance created from tar or petroleum. They are so brittle that usually even one pellet from a shotgun will shatter them.

A NEW PURPOSE

The purpose of trapshooting has changed over the years. It began as a way for hunters to improve their hunting skills. Today, many trapshooters do not hunt. They simply enjoy the sport. No live birds are involved. The last time the Grand American Championship in the United States used live birds was in 1902. Great Britain banned the use of live birds for sport in 1921.

Annie Oakley was one of the most famous shooters of all time.

Trapshooting no longer uses live birds, but some areas of the United States still allow live bird shooting for sport. Animal rights activists and bird lovers across the country are working to stop this practice.

CHAPTER 3

THE BASICS

Trapshooting takes place outdoors. A trap field contains five shooting posts and a structure called a trap house. The trap house is partially buried. The purpose of the trap house is to protect the trap—the machine that releases targets into the air. The trap machine gets its name from the early days of the sport when live birds were released from traps.

Up to five shooters are on the field at a time. One shooter stands at each post. Together, this group of shooters is called a squad. The five shooting posts are spaced three yards (2.7 m) apart and on a slight arc. The closest post is 16 yards (15 m) from the trap house. When shooters look out onto the field, they see the trap house in front of them.

Clay targets are loaded into a trap machine before they can be used.

Watch
for the
striking blade!

ROUNDS

During competition, each member of the squad shoots at one target from each of the five posts. Only one shot is taken at a time. The shooter who starts at Post 1 is the squad leader. He or she yells "Pull!" to indicate being ready for the release of the target. As the target flies through the sky, the shooter takes one shot. Then the shooter at the second post calls for the release of a target. This pattern continues until all five shooters have taken one shot.

After all shooters have taken one shot, the shooter at Post 1 begins the process again for the second round. Once each shooter has taken five shots from his or her initial post, each person in the squad rotates to the next post. The squad leader, now on Post 2, watches to make sure the other shooters are ready for the next round before beginning. No matter which post the squad leader is on, he or she will always be the first to shoot after moving. Each squad member shoots five times from each post. This adds up to a total of 25 shots per round. Rounds take approximately 12 to 15 minutes to complete.

TARGETS

Trapshooting involves releasing targets in the opposite direction of, or away from, the shooter. Standard targets are 4.25 inches (10.8 cm) in diameter. They fly at predictable heights but at unknown angles. The trap machine moves back and forth so shooters won't know exactly where the target will fly. Targets come in a variety of colors, although orange targets are the most common. Targets need to be visible against the background.

In official trapshooting, the trap throws the disc between 49 and 51 yards (45 and 47 m). It also releases the target so it is between 8 and 10 feet (2.5 and 3 m) high when it passes a particular point on the field. These regulations keep the sport fair and help shooters have a basic knowledge of the target's location.

KEEPING SCORE

In a trapshooting competition, the official score is kept by a referee or scorer. Shooters aim to break the target with the shot from their shotguns. It does not matter if the shooter breaks only a small piece from the target or shatters it completely. A point is awarded if any part of the target breaks. Referees rule whether a target either is dead (hit) or a loss (not hit).

TYPES OF TRAP

American trap is divided into three categories. They are singles, doubles, and handicap. Some

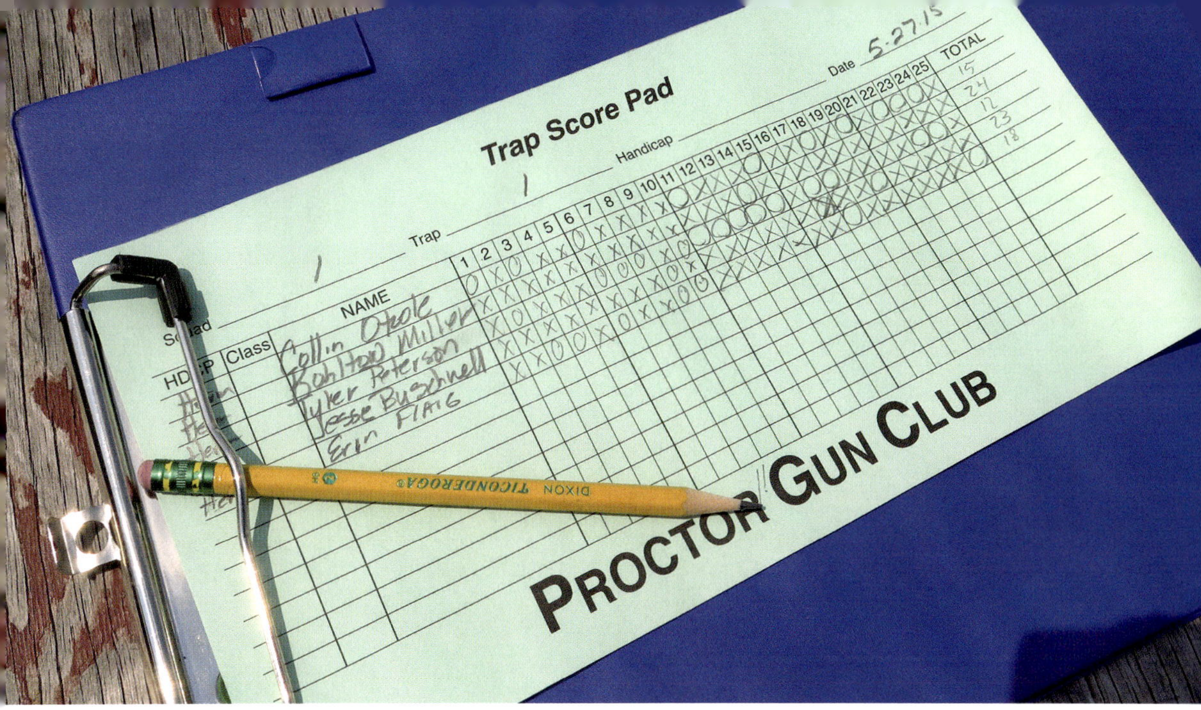

Scores are tallied on a scoresheet as the competition progresses.

competitors choose to shoot in only one category. Others shoot in all three.

Singles trap is the easiest and most popular of the three categories. In singles trap, a shooter stands 16 yards (15 m) from the trap house. This is the front line of the trap field. Shooters are assigned to a five-person squad. The squad rotates through each of the posts. Each member of the squad takes turns shooting five shots from each post. The entire squad then rotates to a different trap field. By the end of the competition, each participant will have shot 100 times

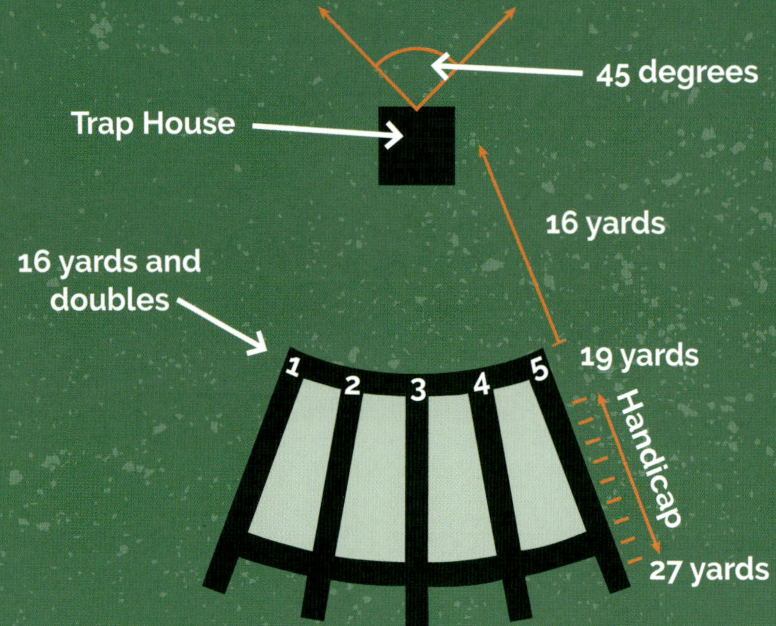

on up to four different trap fields. This group of fields is called a bank.

DOUBLES

In doubles trap, a single shooter aims to break two targets. The targets are shot from the trap house at the same time. One target is shot to the left, and the other is shot to the right. Shooters try to break both targets before they hit the ground. A complete round involves five pairs from each of the five posts. This is a total of 50 targets. As in singles trap, shooters stand at the 16-yard line.

HANDICAP

The third category strives to make the competition as equal as possible. In handicap trap, instead of all shooters standing at the 16-yard line, competitors stand at different distances based on their skill level. The distance is determined by a shooter's scores and placement in earlier events. The most skilled competitors stand the farthest away—up to 27 yards (25 m) from the trap house. The least skilled shooters stand the closest. For men, most beginning shooters start at the 20-yard (18-m) line. Boys aged 14 and under and all women start at the 19-yard (17-m) line. Regardless of where they stand, new shooters should not expect to hit every target.

CHAPTER 4

SAFETY AND GEAR

In any sport, it's important to understand and follow the safety guidelines. This is especially important when using dangerous equipment. Guns, like other sports equipment, can be dangerous when not handled properly. Some organizations and clubs require trapshooters to complete safety training. These courses cover gun safety, protective gear, and trapshooting etiquette.

With proper training and precautions, trapshooting is an extremely safe sport for youths. Between 2001 and 2018, there were no reported injuries in the USA High School Clay Target League. Safety is the number one priority.

Trapshooters should never point their guns at anything but a target.

SAFETY GUIDELINES

Competitors need to be responsible on and off the field. Guns should be handled with care. Some commonsense safety rules help protect all competitors:

- Handle guns only with adult supervision.

- Lock guns when not in use.

- Be aware of surroundings and other people.

- Never point the gun at anything but the clay target, even when the gun is unloaded.

- If the gun has a safety, keep it on until the gun is ready to be fired.

- Keep guns unloaded when not in use.

- Always wear eye and ear protection.

Gun clubs, ranges, and organized shoots all have their own safety policies and procedures. Shooters should always check the rules well before stepping onto the field. Rules violations can result in penalties, suspensions, and bans.

Laws covering minors and firearms vary from state to state. Youths interested in trapshooting should ask adults for help in researching local gun laws.

SHOTGUNS

At the basic level, trapshooting requires very little equipment. Athletes need a shotgun, ammunition, hearing protection, and safety glasses.

Shotguns come in different styles and sizes. Styles include over-and-under, pump-action, and semiautomatic. Common sizes include 12-gauge and 20-gauge. The gauge refers to the width of the interior of the gun's barrel, called a bore. A larger numerical gauge refers to a smaller bore. For example, a 20-gauge is smaller than a 12-gauge. The 12-gauge shotgun is the most common size used in trapshooting.

Shotguns can have one barrel or two barrels. A shotgun with two barrels is called a double-barrel shotgun. The most popular double-barrel shotgun used in trapshooting is the over-and-under, which gets its name because one barrel is stacked on top

LOADING OPTIONS

Pump-action and semiautomatic shotguns are single barrel. They are different from one another in the way they are loaded. A pump-action shotgun requires the shooter to pull back the fore-end of the gun and then push it forward in a "pumping" motion. This releases the shell into the barrel. A semiautomatic gun does not require this pumping movement. It simply loads unused shells into the barrel whenever the trigger is pulled.

Shotshells are ejected from a shotgun as the shooter prepares to reload.

of the other. This is in contrast to the side-by-side, which has two barrels sitting next to each other.

It's normal for trapshooters to experiment with different guns. Many young athletes start with smaller gauges and change guns as they grow bigger and stronger. Athletes who compete in multiple events may use different guns for different categories of competition. A shooter who competes in both singles

Shotshells contain pellets that spray out when fired, giving the shooter a better chance of hitting a moving target.

trap and doubles trap may prefer a single-barrel shotgun for singles events and a double-barrel shotgun for doubles.

AMMUNITION

Shotguns get their name from the type of ammunition they use. Shotguns do not shoot bullets. Instead, they fire shotshells. One shotshell contains multiple pellets. The number of pellets depends on the size of the pellet and the size of the load. Together, these pellets are called shot.

Shooting with shot increases the chances of hitting a fast-moving target. It would be extremely difficult to hit a target with a single projectile, such as a bullet. Instead, one shot of a shotgun releases multiple pellets. These pellets cover a wide area. One pellet can break a clay target.

When shot leaves the gun, it spreads out into a funnel pattern. Shooters can slightly control this pattern by adding a choke to the gun. Chokes are screwed into the muzzle of a gun and change the diameter of the shot spray. Chokes can make the diameter larger or smaller.

Like the shotguns themselves, shot also comes in different sizes. The smaller the shot, the more pellets can fit in a shotshell. However, the smaller the pellet, the closer the target needs to be for it to break. Most trapshooters use #8 or #7.5 shot, but just like with guns, shooters experiment within the rules of the shooting game to see what works best for them.

ADDITIONAL EQUIPMENT

Most clubs and competitions require eye and ear protection. Safety glasses protect the shooter from target shards, pellets, or a gun that does not fire correctly. Everyday sunglasses generally do not provide adequate protection. Shooters should look for something that has side guards. Competitive shooters also choose lens colors to enhance their view of the target.

Ear protection is also necessary. Repeated shotgun blasts damage hearing. Earplugs and earmuffs are two good options to protect hearing. Earmuffs for shooting are not the same as the earmuffs people wear in the winter. They look more like large headphones and completely cover the ear. Some people wear both earplugs and earmuffs.

Another popular piece of gear is a vest or bag to hold ammunition while shooting. Competitors may

Shooters take part in a competition.

also wear shooting gloves, a hat, and comfortable,
supportive shoes. Because trapshooting is
an outdoor sport, shooters need to dress for
the weather.

CHAPTER 5

GETTING INVOLVED

Trapshooting is becoming more and more popular among youths in the United States. One reason is that people of all ages, heights, and skill levels can participate. There is no perfect body shape or size. Shooters can start as early as elementary school and compete all the way through college. Trapshooters can compete individually or on teams.

Participation at the high school level is growing quickly. In 2015, just over 9,000 students participated in the USA High School Clay Target League. Three years later, that number jumped to 21,917. That's a 137 percent increase.

People of all ages can enjoy trapshooting.

Many high schools and colleges offer trapshooting as an extracurricular activity.

ORGANIZED SHOOTING

Youths have several ways to participate in competitive trapshooting. Many high schools, colleges, and universities have trapshooting teams.

Youth shooting organizations exist across the country. Kids who are interested in trapshooting in college should get involved in one of these organizations. Many of them offer scholarships to help pay for college educations.

The Scholastic Shooting Sports Foundation (SSSF) is one such organization. SSSF is the national governing body for the Scholastic Clay Target Program (SCTP). The SCTP is the largest clay target program for young shooters in the United States. It sponsors team-based shooting tournaments across the country. It also works to develop skills in leadership, safe firearm handling, and teamwork.

The Amateur Trapshooting Association (ATA) is another organization. The ATA is the official governing body of American trap. At least 1,000 gun clubs around the country are associated with the ATA. The organization was founded in 1900 as the American Trapshooting Association. Today, it promotes the sport, provides rules and regulations, and develops events and programs.

One of these programs is AIM, which stands for Academics, Integrity, and Marksmanship. It's the official youth program of the ATA. AIM hosts several competitions throughout the year. Participants can compete individually or on teams. Competitors are divided into categories based on their age. The youngest category is Pre-Sub (ages 11 and under), and the oldest is Junior Gold (ages 18 to 22).

TRAP IN SCHOOL

Trap's rising popularity brings unique challenges. One challenge is related to gun control. Gun control is a hot topic in the United States. People have many different opinions about where and how guns should be used. Some think

Trapshooting has been growing in popularity with teenagers.

Shooting sports used to be reserved only for adults, but that is no longer the case.

children should never use guns. Others feel guns are fine when used for sport.

The National Rifle Association (NRA) is very active in this conversation. The NRA is a large supporter of scholastic sports shooting. It provides grants and programs for youth shooters. Many trapshooters are thankful for the NRA's support. Others feel uncomfortable because of the NRA's involvement in politics.

People also have different opinions about trap as a school sport or extracurricular activity, like softball or track and field. There are many questions still being answered. Should guns be allowed in yearbook photos? If so, what kinds of guns? Parents, lawmakers, and school administrators will continue to have these conversations for years to come.

CHAPTER 6

GLOBAL COMPETITION

Shooting has been part of the Olympic Games since the first modern Olympics in 1896. The types of shooting events have changed over the years. At first, women and men competed against one another. The events weren't separated until 1996.

However, a new shooting event called trap mixed was added for the 2020 Olympic Games in Tokyo, Japan. In trap mixed, a man and a woman compete together as a team. Trap mixed replaced the men's doubles trap event. The change was made in an attempt to achieve more gender equality at the Olympic Games.

Trap mixed was added to the 2020 Olympics in Tokyo.

People who use wheelchairs have found increased opportunities to participate in shooting sports.

INTERNATIONAL TRAP

The trapshooting that takes place at the Olympics is different from American trap. It is called Olympic trap, bunker trap, or international trap. Olympic trap is more challenging than American trap. It has different rules. In American trap, all targets are released from a single trap machine. In Olympic trap, targets are released from 15 different trap machines, three at each shooting post. To make it even more challenging, the machines are placed in a bunker in front and are unseen by the shooters behind them.

Additionally, the targets in Olympic trap fly much faster than the targets in American trap. In Olympic trap, the targets fly up to 62 miles per hour (100 km/h). This is compared to 42 miles per hour (68 km/h) in American trap. However, because the target must travel a required distance, that speed is variable depending on the wind conditions and height the target is thrown.

A third difference between the two versions is the number of shots allowed. In American trap, shooters in the singles game get only one shot per target. In Olympic trap, the shooter can shoot at the same target two times. The score is the same whether the target is hit on the first shot or the second shot. Finally, in international trap, athletes rotate through six posts after every shot.

People with physical disabilities also compete in trap on an international level. Paralympic trap was adopted by the World Shooting Para Sports in 2017. The first Para Trapshooting World Championships took place in Italy in 2018.

THE GRAND AMERICAN

American trap is also played on an international level. Athletes from around the world compete in American trap at the Grand American World Trapshooting Championships. The Grand American is the ATA's biggest competition. It's held every August at the World Shooting and Recreational Complex in Sparta, Illinois. The complex has 120 trap fields. It's the longest line

Kim Rhode is one of the most successful shooters in US Olympic history.

of trap fields in the world. The complex is open to the public.

The future of trapshooting is an exciting one. It is a sport with a rich history, but it continues to adapt to the changing times. As trapshooting grows in popularity, new chapters will be added to the sport's ongoing legacy.

GLOSSARY

bank
A group of trap fields used in a shoot.

bore
The interior of the barrel of a gun.

choke
A constraint added to the muzzle of a shotgun to shape the shot pattern.

dead
A target broken by a shooter.

gauge
The interior width of the barrel of the shotgun.

loss
A missed target.

shell
A cartridge that holds the shot.

shot
Small pellets that are projected out of a shotgun.

squad
A group of shooters who shoot together at an event.

trap
The machine used to release the target.

trap house
The structure on a trap field that protects the trap.

MORE INFORMATION

BOOKS

Carpenter, Tom. *Hunting*. Minneapolis, MN: Abdo Publishing, 2020.

Cashin, John. *Firearms Safety*. Pittsburgh, PA: Eldorado Ink, 2014.

ONLINE RESOURCES

To learn more about trapshooting, please visit **abdobooklinks.com** or scan this QR code. These links are routinely monitored and updated to provide the most current information available.

INDEX

Amateur Trapshooting Association (ATA), 35
ammunition, 28–29

Cincinnati, Ohio, 10
Cody, Buffalo Bill, 12
competition procedures, 16–21, 42–43

doubles trap, 20–21, 28, 40

ear protection, 30

field layout, 14, 20

Grain Valley, Missouri, 21
Grand American World Trapshooting Championships, 12, 44–45

handicap, 21
history, 8–12

Ligowsky, George, 11–12

Miller, Dave, 21

National Rifle Association (NRA), 38

Oakley, Annie, 12
Olympics, 7, 40–43, 44

Para Trapshooting World Championships, 44

Rhode, Kim, 44
rules, 18–21, 43

safety glasses, 30
safety tips, 22–25
Scholastic Shooting Sports Foundation (SSSF), 35
scoring, 18, 43
shotguns, 26–28
singles trap, 19–20, 28, 43
skeet shooting, 7, 44
Sparta, Illinois, 44
sporting clays, 7

targets
    birds as, 8–13
    clay, 11–12, 17
    other types, 11
trap mixed, 40

USA High School Clay Target League, 22, 32, 36

ABOUT THE AUTHOR

K. A. Artanne surrounds herself with books, whether she's reading them, writing them, or recommending them to children and teens at the library. She lives in Ohio.